FAMOUS LIVE

STANLEY SCHOOL

Writers

Peggy Burns

HODDER
Wayland

an imprint of Hodder Children's Books

FAMOUS LIVES

Kings and Queens
Saints
Inventors
Explorers
Artists
Engineers
Writers
Campaigners for Change

Series Editor: Alex Woolf
Book Editor: Liz Harman
Designer: Joyce Chester
Consultant: Norah Granger

First published in Great Britain in 1997 by
Wayland (Publishers) Ltd
Reprinted in 2000 by Hodder Wayland,
an imprint of Hodder Children's Books

© Hodder Wayland 1997

Hodder Children's Books, a division of Hodder Headline,
338 Euston Road, London NW1 3BH

British Library Cataloguing in Publication Data

Burns, Peggy, 1941–
 Writers. – (Famous lives)
 1. Novelists, English – Biography – Juvenile
 literature
 2. Women novelists, English – Biography – Juvenile
 literature
 I. Title
 823'.009

ISBN 0 7502 2599 8

Typeset by Joyce Chester
Printed by EUROGRAFICA, Marano, Italy

Picture Acknowledgements

The publishers would like to thank the following for allowing their pictures to be used in this book:
Camera Press cover (top left), cover (background) and 2–3 (background), 26; The Hulton Getty Picture Collection 4 and 28 (top), 5, 8 and 28 (middle), 16 and 29 (middle), 24; Mary Evans 6, 7; The National Trust cover (bottom left), 15 and 28 (bottom); Rex Features 29 (bottom); Topham Picturepoint 22
pages 10 and 11 – line illustrations from THE WIND IN THE WILLOWS copyright E. H. Shepard under the Berne Convention, colouring copyright © 1970, 1971 by E. H. Shepard & Methuen Children's Books. Reproduced by permission of Curtis Brown, London; page 12 – courtesy of the Victoria and Albert Museum; page 13 (top) – Copyright © F. Warne & Co. 1972; page 13 (bottom) – Copyright © F. Warne & Co. 1908, 1987; page 14 – Copyright © F. Warne & Co. 1902, 1987; page 17 (top) – By Courtesy of the National Portrait Gallery, London; pages 17 and 19 – line illustrations from THE HOUSE AT POOH CORNER copyright E. H. Shepard under the Berne Convention, colouring copyright © 1970, 1974 by E. H. Shepard & Methuen Children's Books. Reproduced by permission of Curtis Brown, London. Transparency courtesy of Reed Books; page 18 – line illustration from WINNIE-THE-POOH copyright E. H. Shepard under the Berne Convention, colouring copyright © 1970, 1973 by E. H. Shepard & Methuen Children's Books. Reproduced by permission of Curtis Brown, London. Transparency courtesy of Reed Books; page 23 – cover of *Five on a Treasure Island* by Enid Blyton reproduced by permission of Hodder & Stoughton Limited; cover (right) and page 29 (top), pages 3 and 21, page 20 – © Enid Blyton Limited All Rights Reserved; page 25 – jacket illustration from *Charlie & the Chocolate Factory* (1995 edition) by Roald Dahl, copyright © Quentin Blake, reproduced by permission of Penguin Books Ltd.; page 27 – jacket illustration of *The BFG* reproduced by courtesy of the estate of the author, Roald Dahl, the illustrator, Quentin Blake, and the publisher, Jonathan Cape

Contents

Lewis Carroll

Lewis Carroll's real name was Charles Lutwidge Dodgson. He had seven sisters and three brothers. The children had few friends except for each other.

Charles was very shy when he was not with his family. He had a bad stammer when he spoke.

When he was 14 years old, Charles Dodgson was sent to a boarding school. He hated it there. School bullies made fun of his stammer. They teased him because he was so shy. In spite of this, he did well. He was very good at arithmetic.

◁ *Charles Dodgson, who wrote stories for adults as well as books for children.*

DATES

1832 Birth of Charles Dodgson (Lewis Carroll)
1865 *Alice's Adventures in Wonderland* is published
1898 Death of Charles Dodgson

Alice Liddell, the little girl who gave Charles the idea for his 'Alice' stories. ▷

When he grew up, Charles Dodgson taught arithmetic at Oxford University.

Charles was fond of children. His friend Henry Liddell had three little girls, called Alice, Lorina and Edith. Charles got to know the children, and told them stories.

One day, Charles and Henry took the Liddell children out for a picnic. Charles told them a fairy-tale about a little girl called Alice. In the story, Alice fell into a rabbit hole and found herself in Wonderland.

Alice Liddell loved listening to Alice's adventures. She asked Charles Dodgson to write the stories for her. He called them *Alice's Adventures in Wonderland*.

Charles showed his stories to a publisher. The publisher liked the stories and printed them in a book. Charles Dodgson made up the name 'Lewis Carroll' to call himself on the cover of the book.

Alice in Wonderland was a great success, and Charles Dodgson became very famous. He wrote another book about Alice's adventures, called *Alice Through The Looking Glass*.

◁ *An artist called John Tenniel drew the pictures for* Alice's Adventures in Wonderland.

△ *Alice with some of the animals she meets during her adventures.*

Kenneth Grahame

Kenneth Grahame had two brothers and a sister. Their mother died when Kenneth was only five years old. Their father could not look after the children by himself. He sent them to live many miles away with their grandmother.

◁ Kenneth Grahame.

DATES

1859 Birth of Kenneth Grahame

1908 *The Wind in the Willows*, by Kenneth Grahame, is published

1932 Death of Kenneth Grahame

When he was nine, Kenneth's uncle sent him to a boarding school in Oxford. Kenneth was fond of wildlife. He often sat quietly on the bank of a nearby river, watching the animals.

When Kenneth Grahame left school he wanted to go to university. His family could not afford to pay for him to go. Instead, his uncle got him a job at the Bank of England in London.

Kenneth did not like his job at the bank, but he worked hard. He was very good at his work. In fact, he was given the important job of Secretary of the Bank of England.

Kenneth married a woman called Elspeth. They had one child, a son called Alastair.

Alastair Grahame, the son of Kenneth Grahame. Alastair's parents gave him the nick-name 'Mouse'. ▷

△ *The illustrations for* The Wind in the Willows *were drawn by Ernest Shepard.*

Alastair enjoyed listening to the stories his father told him every night at bedtime. Most of the stories were about the animals Kenneth had seen by the river when he was a little boy.

Kenneth Grahame wrote down his stories of the adventures of Rat, Mole, Badger and the bold and cheeky Toad. He put the animal stories together in a book, called *The Wind in the Willows*.

When *The Wind in the Willows* was first published, adults made fun of it. They thought it was a very silly book. But children everywhere loved the book and it is still read and enjoyed by children today.

Mole and Ratty have to look after Toad, who is always getting into trouble. ▷

▷ *Badger, Mole and Ratty try to make Toad behave sensibly.*

Beatrix Potter

As a little girl, Beatrix Potter was sometimes lonely. She was very fond of her brother, Bertram, but he was away at boarding school. A teacher taught Beatrix at home, so she did not have school friends to play with.

Instead, Beatrix spent her spare time watching animals. She studied beetles, hedgehogs, caterpillars and birds. Beatrix was very good at drawing. She drew pictures of everything she saw.

DATES

1866 Birth of Beatrix Potter
1901 Beatrix Potter's first book, *The Tale of Peter Rabbit*, is published
1943 Death of Beatrix Potter

◁ *Beatrix Potter, aged 15, with her dog, Spot.*

◁ *A page from Beatrix's sketch book. She did these drawings when she was about ten years old.*

Beatrix drew this picture for her book called The Tale of Jemima Puddle Duck. ▽

Beatrix liked writing letters, too. When she grew up, she wrote to her teacher's children. The letters told the stories of Peter Rabbit, Squirrel Nutkin and many other animals. Beatrix drew little pictures of the animals all over the letters.

The children enjoyed the stories, so Beatrix decided to send them to a publisher. He liked them. Beatrix was thrilled when her first little book, *The Tale of Peter Rabbit*, was published.

Beatrix worked very hard, and wrote more books, all with her own beautiful pictures in them. She and her publisher, Norman Warne, became good friends. They decided to get married. Sadly, Norman died before the wedding.

When Beatrix's aunt died, she left Beatrix some money. Beatrix used the money to buy a small farm, called Hill Top, in the Lake District.

△ *Peter Rabbit, the naughty rabbit who stole radishes from Mr McGregor's garden.*

Beatrix Potter became famous for her books. But the farm kept her busy. She had less and less time to write and draw and, in time, she stopped writing.

Beatrix Potter's books are still loved by adults as well as children.

△ Beatrix Potter standing outside Hill Top Farm.

Alan Alexander Milne

Alan Alexander Milne loved to write. When he was a little boy he wrote some stories and sent them to a children's newspaper. They were not printed, but Alan went on writing anyway.

When he grew up, Alan studied arithmetic at Cambridge University. His father hoped that Alan would get a really good job. But all Alan wanted to do was write. He decided to try to earn a living from writing. His father was very upset.

DATES

1882 Birth of Alan Alexander Milne
1926 Alan Alexander Milne writes *Winnie-the-Pooh*
1956 Death of Alan Alexander Milne

◁ *Alan Alexander Milne.*

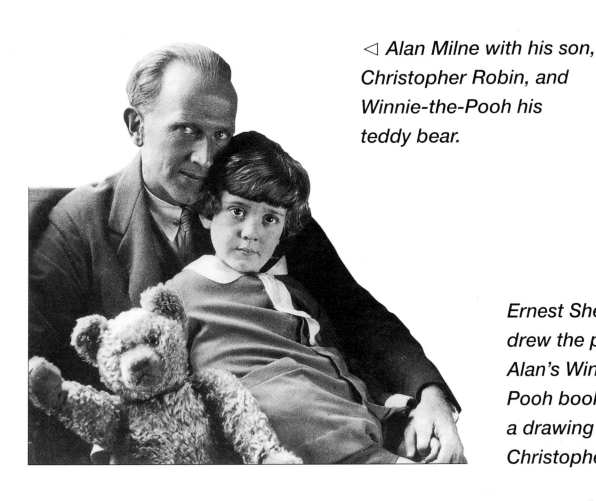

◁ Alan Milne with his son, Christopher Robin, and Winnie-the-Pooh his teddy bear.

Ernest Shepard drew the pictures for Alan's Winnie-the-Pooh books. This is a drawing of Christopher Robin. ▽

Alan Milne was not able to sell any of his writing for a very long time. Life was very hard. At last, he got a job writing for a magazine called *Punch*.

Alan had a son, called Christopher Robin. Alan began to write stories about Christopher Robin and his teddy bear, Winnie-the-Pooh. Christopher Robin's other toys – Tigger the tiger, Eeyore the donkey and Piglet – were also in the stories.

Alan's children's stories were published. His writing became very popular. He wrote books, plays and poems for adults and children. Some of the children's poems were also about Christopher Robin.

When Christopher Robin was older, the other children at school made fun of him because of the stories and verses his father had written about him.

△ *Winnie-the-Pooh and his friend Piglet have lots of adventures together.*

△ *Winnie-the-Pooh and Piglet with some of the other animals in A. A. Milne's stories – Tigger, Kanga and Roo, Owl, Rabbit and Eeyore.*

It is now 70 years since A. A. Milne wrote the Winnie-the-Pooh stories but Pooh is still the teddy bear children like to read about. The Winnie-the-Pooh stories have even been made into animated films.

Enid Blyton

Enid Blyton was a teenager when she began writing. When she was just 14 years old she won first prize in a poetry competition.

Enid was still a young girl when her parents quarrelled. Her father left the house. Enid and her two brothers lived at home with their mother.

◁ *Enid Blyton with her two daughters, Gillian and Imogen.*

Enid wrote lots of stories about Noddy, the little man with a bell on his hat. This is a picture of Noddy in his car, with his friend Big Ears. ▷

Enid liked children and, when she was 19, she became a teacher. She still found time to write stories. Before long, children began to write letters to her, telling her how much they liked her books. Soon she was getting hundreds of letters every week.

Some of Enid Blyton's books were for adults, but most of all she liked writing children's stories. She said that if she didn't have to eat and sleep in between, she could write a whole book without stopping! She wrote a lot of books for her own two daughters, Gillian and Imogen.

△ *Enid at work, typing her stories.*

Enid wrote circus stories, school stories, books about rabbits, fairies and naughty toys. She also wrote books of prayers and poems. Some of Enid's most famous stories are about the adventures of the Secret Seven and the Famous Five.

DATES

1897 Birth of Enid Blyton
1949 Enid Blyton writes her first Noddy story
1968 Death of Enid Blyton

The cover of one of Enid's Famous Five stories. The Famous Five were four children – Julian, Dick, Anne and George the tomboy – and Timmy the dog. ▽

Enid Blyton wrote more than 700 books. She became the most successful children's writer in Britain. Her books have been printed in many different languages. Five hundred million of her books have been sold all over the world.

Roald Dahl

Roald Dahl's parents were born in Norway but moved to Britain, where Roald and his brothers and sisters grew up.

During the Second World War, Roald Dahl became a pilot. He flew fighter planes. One day his plane crashed. He managed to crawl out before it exploded, but he was badly hurt.
He had bad headaches and pain in his back for the rest of his life.

△ Roald Dahl, his wife, Patricia and three of their children with their nanny.

After the war, Roald became a writer.
Roald and his wife Patricia had five children
– Olivia, Tessa, Theo, Ophelia and Lucy.
Every night, Roald told the children
a different bedtime story. Sadly, Olivia died
when she was seven years old.

△ Charlie and The
Chocolate Factory *is one of
Roald Dahl's most popular
books. Like many of his
books, it was illustrated by
Quentin Blake.*

△ *Roald Dahl at work in his office.*

Roald Dahl wrote more than 30 books. Most of them were for children. Children like his books because they are exciting and often very funny.

Roald's office was a wooden hut in the garden. He did not use a typewriter. Instead, he wrote all his stories with a pencil. He would sit in an old armchair with his legs tucked inside a cosy sleeping bag.

Many of Roald Dahl's children's books have been made into films. He did not think the films were very good.

Roald Dahl died in 1990. His books are still very popular. *James and the Giant Peach* and *Fantastic Mr Fox* are great favourites.

Roald thought that The BFG *was his very best book. It is about a big, friendly giant. Roald wrote the book in memory of his little girl, Olivia.* ▽

DATES

1916 Birth of Roald Dahl
1982 Dahl writes *The BFG*
1990 Death of Roald Dahl

Timeline

Year	Writer	How long ago?
1830		170 years ago
1832	Lewis Carroll (Charles Lutwidge Dodgson) born in Cheshire, England	
1840		160 years ago
1850		150 years ago
1859	Kenneth Grahame born in Scotland	
1860		140 years ago
1864	Kenneth Grahame is sent to live with his grandmother after his mother's death	
1865	*Alice's Adventures in Wonderland*, by Lewis Carroll, is published	
1866	Beatrix Potter born in London	
1870		130 years ago
1880		120 years ago
1882	Alan Alexander Milne born	
1890		110 years ago
1897	Enid Blyton born in London	
1898	Death of Lewis Carroll	
1898	Kenneth Grahame becomes Secretary of the Bank of England	
1900		100 years ago
1905	Beatrix Potter buys Hill Top Farm	

Year	Writer	How long ago?
1910		90 years ago
1916	Roald Dahl born in Cardiff, South Wales	
1920		80 years ago
1920	Christopher Robin Milne born	
1922	Enid Blyton's first book, a book of poems, is published	
1930		70 years ago
1932	Death of Kenneth Grahame	
1940		60 years ago
1943	Death of Beatrix Potter	
1950		50 years ago
1956	Death of Alan Alexander Milne	
1960		40 years ago
1964	Roald Dahl's book *Charlie and The Chocolate Factory* is published	
1968	Death of Enid Blyton	
1970		30 years ago
1980		20 years ago
1990	Death of Roald Dahl	10 years ago

Words to look up

animated film a moving film which is made up of many drawings, rather than pictures of real people and things

arithmetic a type of mathematics, a way of working with numbers

boarding school a school where children live most of the time

bullies people who are unkind to other people and sometimes hurt them

competition an activity in which people try to do better than other people

exploded blew up

illustrations pictures or drawings that appear in books

magazine a type of newspaper with stories and articles, usually written by different people

nanny a person who looks after children

pilot a person who flies a plane

poems pieces of text that rhyme or have a rhythm

prayers words said when talking to God

publisher a person or a company who prints books to sell in shops

stammer to pause or say a sound over and over while speaking

university a place where adults go to study different subjects

Some places to see

The Ashdown Forest, West Sussex – where A. A. Milne's Winnie-the-Pooh stories are set. You can visit The Enchanted Place and Pooh Bridge, both mentioned in A. A. Milne's books.

Beatrix Potter Gallery, Hawkshead, Cumbria – an exhibition of Beatrix Potter's illustrations from her children's books, which is changed every year.

Hill Top Farm in Sawrey, Cumbria – Beatrix Potter's farm, which is now owned by the National Trust.

The World of Beatrix Potter, The Old Laundry, Crag Brow, Bowness-on-Windermere, Cumbria – an exhibition, film and shop and the Tailor of Gloucester Tea Room.

Other books to look at

Alice's Adventures in Wonderland by
Lewis Carroll, Methuen 1985

*Through the Looking Glass and What
Alice Found There* by Lewis Carroll,
Andersen Press, 1992

Nonsense Verse by Lewis Carroll,
Ladybird 1995

*The Wind in The Willows – The River
Bank* by Kenneth Grahame, Picture
Lions (Harper Collins) 1996

The Open Road by Kenneth Grahame,
Magnet Paperback 1981

The River Bank by Kenneth Grahame,
Magnet Paperback 1981

Beatrix Potter's stories, including *The
Tailor of Gloucester, The Tale of Peter
Rabbit, The Tale of Squirrel Nutkin,
The Tale of Jemima Puddle Duck* and
The Tale of Benjamin Bunny are

published by Frederick Warne & Co.

When We Were Very Young by A. A.
Milne, Methuen 1989

Now We are Six by A. A. Milne, Methuen
1989

Winnie-the-Pooh by A. A. Milne, Methuen
1973

The House at Pooh Corner by A. A. Milne,
Methuen 1974

Five Minute Tales by Enid Blyton,
Mammoth Publishing, 1992

The Magic Faraway Tree by Enid Blyton,
Mammoth Publishing, 1991

The Folk of the Faraway Tree by Enid
Blyton, Mammoth Publishing 1996

Roald Dahl's books, including *The BFG,
Fantastic Mr Fox, Dirty Beasts* and
Charlie and the Chocolate Factory are
published by Puffin

Index